Zoey's Adventures

A Day at the Lake

Gwendolyn H. Lyle

Fulton Books, Inc.
Meadville, PA

Published by Fulton Books 2020

ISBN 978-1-64952-284-9 (paperback)
ISBN 978-1-64952-285-6 (digital)

Printed in the United States of America

Thank you Reese, for giving me
the time and the rhyme.

Today we are going to play in the lake.

Follow me down the trail.
How long could it take?

We are here at the dock.

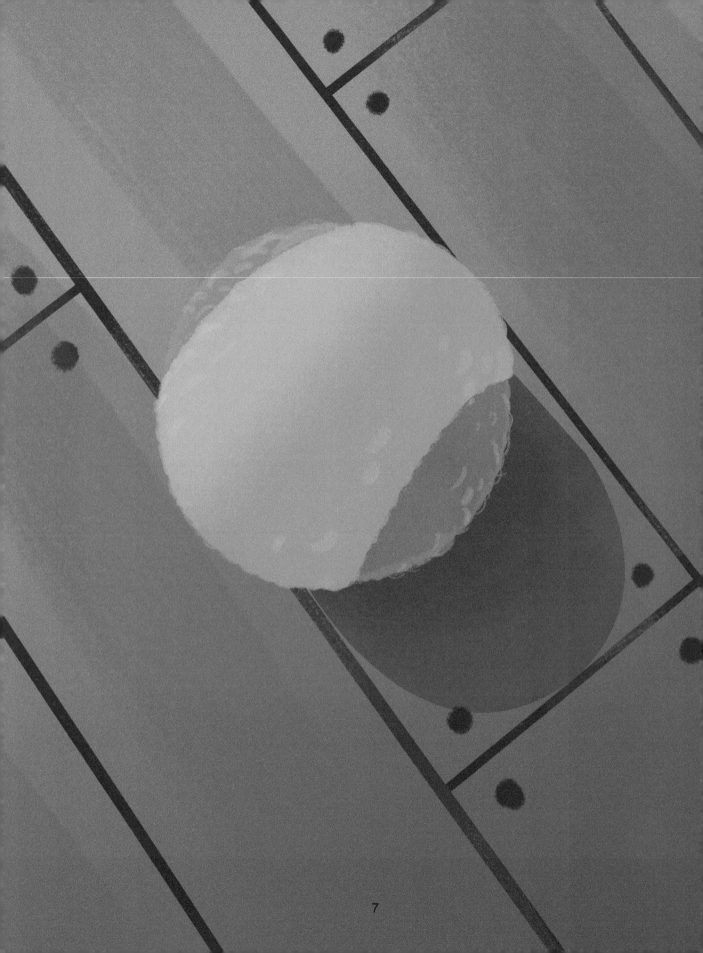

Look, it's a ball!

Let me get on my life jacket.

Here we go, y'all!

I'll swim back to the dock.

And climb up the ladder.

I do hope they'll throw it.

Which way, does not matter.

I love this game; I do like to play.

Fetch is something I can do all day!

About the Author

Gwendolyn is a domestic engineer living on Lake Lanier with her husband of thirty-six years.

Zoey is a Poochon that came into her family as a puppy.

From day one, she would follow Gwendolyn everywhere and do anything she was doing.

She was very entertaining and loved by all.

We hope you enjoy following her adventures as much as we did.

CPSIA information can be obtained
at www.ICGtesting.com
Printed in the USA
LVHW070604160321
681656LV00028B/833

9 781649 522849